THE PORTAGE POETRY SERIES

Series Titles

Not Just the Fire
R.B. Simon

Monarch
Heather Bourbeau

Bone Country
Linda Nemec Foster

The Body is Burden and Delight
Sharon White

The Walk to Cefalù
Lynne Viti

The Found Object Imagines a Life: New and Selected Poems
Mary Catherine Harper

Naming the Ghost
Emily Hockaday

Mourning
Dokubo Melford Goodhead

Messengers of the Gods: New and Selected Poems
Kathryn Gahl

After the 8-Ball
Colleen Alles

Careful Cartography
Devon Bohm

Broken On the Wheel
Barbara Costas-Biggs

Praise for
Not Just the Fire

"At turns harrowing and stunningly graceful, R.B. Simon's latest collection *Not Just the Fire* shows us through her deft and emotionally potent lyricism and spare narratives how 'to touch the flame / while it / [is] still / burning.' With evocative diction and sensory images, these poems are gorgeous and necessary and sing the deep truths and lessons of a warrior who has returned with both the wounds and the wisdom of experience. We readers feel deep in our guts the growth and healing the speaker has undergone throughout her lifetime in these tightly woven verses. I highly recommend."

—Jenn Givhan
author of *Belly to the Brutal*

"From love poems to her eleven-year-old self to her dead lover, from the cruel racism of children to musings about swallowing the galaxy, these poems range from whimsical to somber to an acceptance of decades of hardships that did not defeat. After muted agony, R.B. always returns us to a lover's fingertips stroking her neck, to the playfulness of children building forts, to the body as a site of scars with the promise of tenderness. *Not Just the Fire* is Simon's mesmerizing entry into the literary world. Her astonishing use of language is worth the price of admission alone."

—Chris Stark
author of *Carnival Lights* and *Nickels: A Tale of Dissociation*
Lambda Literary Finalist

"When we find ourselves lost in affliction, how do we find our way out? In her devastating collection, *Not Just the Fire*, R.B. Simon invites us into the painful world of childhood trauma, addiction & grief, of 'cobwebs thick as batwings,' 'a rough country of ancestry.' Through powerful imagery, Simon asks us to consider 'the reason / snakes shed skin.' We meet a mother, partner, and daughter who know the pain of 'clinging / to the crumbling core / of a world…worth saving.' Here is a reckoning with complex identities and family relationships as well as a path into and out of active addiction. Ultimately, Simon conveys what may be the most important truth: that 'the heart / must be pumping / before you can bleed / for anyone,' that to make it through the fire and out alive means that anything & everything is possible."

—Joan Kwon Glass
author of *Night Swim*

Not Just the Fire

Poems

R.B. Simon

Cornerstone Press
Stevens Point, Wisconsin

Cornerstone Press, Stevens Point, Wisconsin 54481
Copyright © 2023 R.B. Simon
www.uwsp.edu/cornerstone

Printed in the United States of America by
Point Print and Design Studio, Stevens Point, Wisconsin

Library of Congress Control Number: 2022947737
ISBN: 979-8-9869663-0-4

Cornerstone Press titles are produced in courses and internships offered by the
Department of English at the University of Wisconsin–Stevens Point.

DIRECTOR & PUBLISHER   EXECUTIVE EDITOR
Dr. Ross K. Tangedal   Jeff Snowbarger

SENIOR EDITORS
Lexie Neeley, Monica Swinick, Kala Buttke

PRESS STAFF
Alyssa Bronk, Grace Dahl, Patrick Fogarty, Angela Green, Cal Henkens, Brett Hill,
Ryan Jensen, Julia Kaufman, Hunter Kiesow, Adam King, Amanda Leibham, Maria
Scherer, Abbi Wasielewski

*For Stephanie T. and Emily H.,
for getting me here through the toughest of times.
With ceaseless gratitude.*

Also by R.B. Simon:

The Good Truth

Poems

(Re)Incarnation

Like all birds, mythical or not,
      there is an egg.

Inside, darkness. Then ember,
         as the fiery sliver
         ignites within its yolk of ash.

Days uncounted, for days are of no
consequence, curled as they are
      in endless coils.

It is no easy thing, birthing, when all
you remember is the sweltering dark;

Yet driven by the body's demand for burning,
white-hot beak demanding exit,
   a sudden influx of oxygen as flaming wings spread wide,
      at once aloft.

In the end, what makes you a phoenix is not
just the fire,
      but the flight.

metamorphosis

entombed
in a battered cocoon
one elbow thrust
through a raw cut at defiant angle
pinpricks of daylight scalding
one newborn eye
the other still weepily
painted shut
furtive frantic wriggling
stopped mid-motion
at sensed approach
bound and blind
moment hung on
one endless breath
at last released
to praise the blade
that freed you

Snow Fort

those bright white days
when the new snow glazed the city in innocence,
we'd package ourselves, brittle Christmas bulbs
in layers of socks, long underwear, sweats, jeans,
and spill out the front door whooping
with the rarity of freedom.
snow smooshed by penguined hands
into the likeness of medieval bricks
piled into tiers and towers,
we hid behind the U-shaped walls
of a barricade with peek-a-boo slits,
amassed pyramids of snowballs
at our big-booted feet, lobbed each one
across the shimmering expanse,
ribs forced outward by our laboring lungs
until, sun buried, we clomped up slick stairs
peppered with mud from the threadbare yard,
chunky with salt, our throats icy and raw
as we peeled off the crusted armor,
sank into rough-worn sofa cushions
and pleaded for Swiss Miss,
wrapped mugs around mugs, slurping
only the mini marshmallows,
before falling asleep
a pile of pups in soggy long johns.

dreams, for once, easy,
salved
by a snow-laden day.

Ideas on Surviving

The night seeps in, locks and codes on a cellular level. The black aches in my bones like a miasma, becomes the shame I've kept hidden like the box of chocolates I eat stealthily in a closet at 2 in the morning. Who do I think I am fooling with my survival, when everyone ought to know that I shattered the moment my 5-year-old hand was swallowed up in my grandfather's guiding grasp? My blood turns tar in a swirling cyclone of disgrace. My literacy for breathing is nothing less than a miracle, the in-and-out a testament to overcoming mortification in its infinite forms, my humiliation calibrated to annihilate like a biological imperative. My life is a weeping clockwork, but at least in motion, hands dragging a millisecond at a time towards the inexorable end scene, days passed posed in an anxious gaping trying to eke living into the frame. Part of my name means forever just like part of my name means rebirth; forever dying and forever reborn again from the ashes but not like the proverbial phoenix as much as the unkempt coal of a banked fire which ignites a passing leaf, flaming to radiant, temporary life.

Molt

I know the reason
snakes shed skin,
and crabs forsake shells
on forgotten coasts
to fill with water and float away
like storm-wracked boats.
Carapace grown too tight,
world within grown larger
than the world beyond.

I know the despair
of counting all the stars
in the night sky attempting to
hold back the maddening clamor
of my thoughts. Thinking,
if I could reach out just one hand,
pluck a single brightness
down to wish upon, I would beg
to be rebirthed as a creature
who can live without skin.

Traditions

My mama, white as the porcelain
bird she kept on the shelf in the living room,
my mama crooned me lullabies, stroked my hair,
rings of silky curls, never nappy like daddy's,
my mama fanned my locks across the corduroy pillow,
sang in her sweet lilt of everlasting mama love.

    She never sang me gospel songs,
    never taught me of my ancestors.

My mama taught me all people are created the same.
She said we should be color-blind, all blood runs red.
My mama was a feminist, told me women deserved the same pay as me
My mama taught me to fight for civil rights for gays,
for anyone different from me,
but never to see differences.

    She never made me soul food,
    never cooked me collard greens or grits.

My mama taught me "proper" English
because it was all she knew how to speak.
My mama insisted I learn to pay attention:
how billboards used women's bodies to sell cars,
how they marketed tennis shoes to young black men
who couldn't afford them, using metaphors of war.

    She never told me the stories of Nefertiti or Langston or Rosa,
    never showed me any footprints to follow but her own.

My mama defied her entire clan to marry outside her race
at the ripe old age of eighteen, dared miscegenation.

My mama was disowned by the richest, brightest branches of our family tree, became the whitest of black sheep, then skulked home to a brooding mother, hungry babe in arms when that no-good negro ran off with the next blonde lady.

She never told me a black man had broken her heart.

She never had to.

The House I Lived In

What we speak becomes the house we live i
—Hafi

I walk the seven blocks alone down Hackett Street,
towards my daily stop for binge food at Liberty Pharmacy,
before hanging a left on Middle Street and the last five blocks to home

Inside I run a litany
counting the remaining steps:

59 I'm such a burden
58 No one likes me
57 My face is uneven
56 My legs are so fat

until I'm swallowed into the safety
of pulled curtains and an empty house.

How many prizes in my paper bag –
how many seconds until the satiation of

HoHos and Suzy Qs and Ding Dongs, first licked clean of frosting
then eaten in gulping bites of cream and cake, drowning out
my numbered failures with my own laboring mandibles.

Next, the clamor of a TV volume cranked for cover, the echoing
retching from the tiny pink half-bath off my father's study,
a hiss of air freshener masking the evidence.

My father arrived home every day at quarter after five.
By that time, I was always upstairs in my room.
He would head for his study, continue with his workday.

We stayed two floors apart.

schools

round-shouldered on a windless day, alone on the swing set,
little brown girl hangs, toe tips scratching blacktop.
she pretends not to notice the approach of the predators.

hey! they call. they know her name, but never use it.
heat floods her face like boiling water, pavement so hot vapor zig-zags
across the concrete field as schoolchildren mill in pods

screeching and laughing in games of tag and kickball,
the amoeba-like pattern of them netting the full attention
of the teacher who never sees her.

hey, brown crayon! burnt toast! what's the matter?
did you know your mama left you in the oven too long?
taunts sting like electric eels across the back of her neck.

they surround her, the piranhas of the playground, as she wonders
if she will stand or bolt. heat and resignation hold her fast.
there is no more sanctuary in the school than in the wide world she flees.

hey, nigger-girl, where you from? africa? why you come here?
she has no answers for them, never answers, has learned the hard way
it's better to remain silent than hook her own mouth on defense.

tears prick, but she clamps her eyes defiantly. oh look!
zebra girl is gonna cry! laughter ripples through the group.
the stinging behind her orange-lit eyelids grows.

she stands, opening her eyes to slits to find a way through,
sees none. her feet melt to the pavement, dismayed.
laughter wells up again, closer now, they are tightening the circle.

panic belches up, then a jolt – the shrill of the recess bell.
she stays, rooted like seaweed, until all the kids have run inside,
then drags her heavy body through the thick embarrassment.

returning to the door, a teacher awaits her, scowling.
'you are always so slow! why don't you exercise?' she knows
she cannot win their games, but nods, and follows the current.

Eight Facets of My Step-Father

Working.
Barricaded in his first-floor den,
wooden louvered-door cabinets
hung shadowed
above his silent round-shouldered form
scritching, shuffling papers,
absentmindedly stroking bushy beard,
curly auburn hair shaken by rare huffs
of surprise or laughter.
I did not need to see his taciturn face.
I knew not to disturb him.

Holidays.
Joyless trepidation paired with practiced smiles.
Stoically opening his presents,
me wary and wondering, still as ice.
I looked for his return gift, still surprised by the drop
of disappointment at his store-bought card
with meaningless promises of a home-made gift.

Weekdays.
After school, the house a mausoleum,
frozen hush shattered only by sobs
from the upstairs bathroom,
where my bottom numbed from hours on the toilet.
I'm startled by his gruff staccato
from the other side of the door,
admonishing *you have nothing in your life worth*
crying about.

Junior year.
Coming home to all the louvered cabinets
empty, not even a note, divorcing me along with her.
Mom and I defiantly bought the VCR he said

we could never afford. Each week punctured
by awkward phone calls I didn't know how to end.

Graduation day.
An extravagant gift of luggage,
the irony of him helping me leave not lost.
Dinner at the Chinese restaurant felt thorny,
post-ceremony photos excruciating.

College.
Halting attempts
at phone conversations
came less and less.

Moving.
Packing for the big city,
I didn't call him for help.

My phone.
Silent.

Lanterns

Even in daylight
I bring lanterns
to my psyche's dark corners.
What haunts me there
absorbs all light,
reverse prism
reflections of ghosts
from murkier days,
where cobwebs
thick as batwings
hung in the recesses
of gloomy basements,
dim garages.
Where hands dry as gravel,
scaled with callus and grit,
wandered the soft roselle
of young shoulders,
belly still round with baby fat,
and warning whispers fell
like dying swans,
velvety black,
into chasms,
muted.

Apologies

"If I had my wits about me"
    I mutter to the store clerk,
as if my wits
        had dropped like loose coins
    out of the bottom of my purse
   then landed   along bike paths
      or sidewalks
  bewildered and unclaimed
waiting for me like Bo Peep's errant flock
     to cluck them home to safety.

  If honesty
  were on my lips
I'd confess my wits have
      been flayed   like political prisoners
    wrapped in razor wire
of insecurity, grief,
   until they have hung limp,
  lifeless, useless.

  So when the time comes
  for clever repartee,
    idle chit-chat
     I stutter, apologize,
   my ravaged rabbit-foot wits
    dangling   from a back pocket
  as if for luck
I'll never have.

The Sacrifice

Sweet child,
my breath still catches on the hook of my ribs
when I think of you laid in front of me,
when I think of what the men did to us,
when I think of what I was forced to do to you.
Men shrouded in cloying smoke
covered in your blood
while I stood centered in a ritual star,
six years old, stupefied, sobbing.

No one knows better than I the cost of trading life for life.

I wish I could swear I'd lived life in your honor,
But for so, so long, I didn't.

Yet I sit bundled on my own porch,
one chilly November morning, watching
the sky brighten to yellow-pink streaks
the snot tiny ice slopes ramping from my nose.

The dawn light outlines the carcasses
of the moon-faced lilies I planted last year
whose bulbs I should have tucked in
before winter's firm arrival.
Nothing prepared them
for the hard shock of first frost,
and they've lain dormant,
frozen in unforgiving loam, awaiting
the sun's rescue.

Somehow I am still hopeful
they will survive.

I know that icy earth, bleak moments of waiting,
an unknowing of seasons, the piercing disbelief in daylight's return.

Sweet child,
whose light was ripped away before you could shine,
this too honored you, although I didn't understand
until now.

For when the world spun round again,
and I erupted forth, as pure as that lily,
as innocent, I claimed the sunlight
for us both.

Backpage Baby

phone gripped
in your clammy palm,
you are praying
for it to ding

but also for its silence
because you know the drill
when the messages do come
how to paint your face for their pleasure
bathe yourself in cherry blossom and musk
smother yourself in satin and lace
answer the door
with your most enticing smile fastened on

your mind will be hollow
as you lay down with them
you'll feel no pleasure
feel nothing but absence
your savaged heart mummified
in a shredded baby blanket
your skeleton a jail cell

your thoughts flying
hours ahead
to when the true feeling you crave
plunges down your blazing veins
and you can cease,
finally lay your head against
your love's chest and listen,
until the whole world
is her heartbeat

Grand Prix

It's been a while since your macho southern drawl
coated a "Hey, Sweetie" like engine lube, slicking its way
thru the phone signal to land its way against my warm cheek.
I'd be lying if I said I didn't miss your charm.

You're a fast one. Engine revved and built for speed
and the squeal of smoking tires. But I've lost
my front row seat at the races. Still steadying
from the whiplash of watching you race around
the endless track. I'm gave up hoping you might stay
each time you pulled in for a pit stop.

Just remember – Sweetie –
every engine will burn when the oil overfills.
The pile-up when you crash won't even make the news.

Emily

As if you were given an edict,
your name
meant to strive
and always,
always you were trying to be
some place, some *one* different,
be a person
you had yet to become

Timeworn and watery as the stars
inked on your shoulder,
blackened jellyfish in the sun
burned by everything robbed from you
all that was ripped from your underbelly,
still you shone, my Emily, pearlescent
through turbid waters

You drowned slowly
choked by your chosen poisons,
addicted to the wracking of your body,
preferring to breathe underwater,
emotions diluted, vision blurred

Pulled into your whirlpool,
I watched your stars sink beneath the waves
paralyzed between reaching out to you,
or sinking into the same blessed oblivion

Emily, it was as if you
were given an omen
your name meant
to strive
yet never answered
the question of what towards.

But always, always,
you tried

Eight and a Half Lilies in October

The last words the family spoke to her
were to report they'd thrown away her
flowers from the funeral.
A stunning display of snow-white lilies
in a crystal vase tossed like last night's
takeout. It had been all the money left
after paying for her new apartment,
and when she'd gone to sign the lease,
the landlord insisted on crossing off her newly
deceased lover's name in a big bold line.
For legal reasons.

She bought more lilies the next day.
A dozen huge heads of *lilium candidum*,
one for every month she'd been with her love.
They'd been closer than twins in the womb, inseparable.
Most days they had even showered together.

She watered the flowers daily, and they
shone white as bleached bedsheets.
She imagined them alive forever, an eternal
token, indestructible though they seemed fragile
as her love's shuddering ribs under her palms
the night she cracked downward
in desperate compressions.

On day five, faint brown tinged the outside of one petal.
She removed that flower.

Two days later, a second flower came out of the vase.
Wary now, she began to remove single petals.

One morning, swaying blindly through her morning
routine of meds, coffee, watering the flowers,
she froze. Every sweet, white bloom was marred,
russet stains edging the petals. Her vision
swam with the face of love's mother, gravelly voice
scraping against her memory:

> *You were just another junkie.*
> *She never loved you anyway.*

Grabbing the remaining wilted stems, vase and all,
she swung around wildly and threw them
in the trash. Coffee left half made,
she went back to her empty bed.

Luna

she was the kind of person
　　who faded in the
　　　　sunlight
but glowed
　　luminescent
　　　　　eclipsing the
　　cold ecru of the moon

arms wrapped in silver bangles
　　　slim fingers in silver rings
words etching
　　silver-tongued trails
　　　　in the ears of eager
　　devotees

like malingering moths
　　　her adoring public
　flapped around her　　overlooking
　　　　the blight of despondency
in her ebullient laughter
wanting only
　　　to touch the flame
　　while it
　　　was still
　　　　　burning

Ode to My Track Marks

You live along the side
of my wrists, the crooks
of both elbows, behind the knees

I touch you, gentle as dabbing the gift
of perfume from a new lover

white puckered punctures
echo the urgency of insatiable need
the slick steel sharp a cupid's arrow.

Nostalgia is a jealous ex-lover, begging me
to remember the feral romance of bells
ringing in my blood, explosions of endorphins
shaking my body to seizure.

Yet you, my darling scars, also sing to me of
the bad breakup, shitting and sweating,
the old whore I'd become, a novel

in there-but-for-the-grace-of-god
read in braille across my body

a story ending in your slowly smoothing flesh,
and my dreamless sleep,
pressed against my beloved.

snap/shot

Stoned with grief, awake
still from my nocturnal pursuits,
I stare blankly at her back as she is eaten
by the school's shadowed entryway,
my bruised veins blazing regret.

Gradually, memory prods: *it is the first day*,
and I've forgotten to say *freeze*,
pose her in front of the building,
beg her forced smile.
I grab my cell, swipe the shutter,
just catch her blurry back.

I want to call her back to me,
crave some kind of resuscitation,
life breathed back into the life I birthed.
Instead, I am leaving. My purple suitcase
packed for a rehab bed open in two days.

I stare at the fuzzy photo of her, walking
with long, crisp strides in striped tee and jeans,
her backpack hitched over one denim-jacketed shoulder
as she rushes away from me in converse hi-tops.
Her back is needle straight, stiff with an unplunged rage
    – at a world where fourteen-year-old daughters
    hold their wailing mothers at five in the morning –
    – where mother's lover dies of an overdose
    in the middle of the living room floor –

and still her first day of high school dares to start three weeks late
I slump against the seat, drop the phone beside me.
Silent, head bent to steering wheel in entreaty,
I pray to never again miss a photo of her first day.

She doesn't look back at the car.
Sure of her destination, she walks
steadily away from the trap
of what we once called a home.

Second Harvest

she is such a tiny bud, raw
with winter's scrubbed potential, born to high winds
to parents of dune thistle
grandparents of red baneberry
lost in a rough country of ancestry
not recognizing oak from aspen
from elder

i want to bring her baskets of our fruit
crops of blackberries or little wild strawberries just plump enough
to crush between teeth, to burst open and stain the lips
i want them tart with her lineage,
of whom she was grown to be
of how she was rooted a thousand years ago

and i am no master gardener
unskilled at pruning or coaxing bud to blossom,
i can't tell sly weed from straining sapling
except for this one
glorious shoot

so go ahead, dance, little one
let your bare toes take root everywhere they will,
let the wind shake loose your laughter
like seeds
and let it
settle, fatten, sprout,
and seek new sun

this is no longer
my harvest

De Corde Meo

I too often see with the eyes
of my heart, in adoration
of frangible flesh (slitted
for love of loving) and it
lays me naked   clinging
                      to the crumbling core
of a world I insist is worth saving.

It is far past time I learned
what this organ is for – the sucking
                      in of everything red and sacred,
only to fling it out again to the ends of its realm
with all its valor.

There is no capacity
to measure, no scale to balance.

Only the propulsion of
holy truth – the heart
                  must be pumping
before you can bleed
for anyone, even
yourself.

Animal Behavior

A sturdy white gate sits stretched across our kitchen doorway
placed to separate one single dog from our pack of four.

The youngest pup has become aggressive towards one of the others;
no one can say exactly why his behavior changed.

Once he loped happily alongside his dog brothers;
now he guards food ferociously and attacks at random.

These days he and his sibling have reached such states of anxiety
that neither can react with anything but instant, unreasoned violence.

Trainers and treats, dog park excursions to the point of exhaustion,
nothing has calmed them enough to tolerate each other.

I want to explain to him that this is his tribe,
they are a pack, meant to tumble and snuggle together.

As time passes, we know we must choose peace, which means
choosing among the equally beloved, between brothers.

For now, the gate remains.

Pandemic Dreams

I don't know if you understand me when I say
that humans are pack animals.
I mean last year it was OK to touch my fingertips
casually to someone's arm as we talked.
Do you feel like an astronaut now,
bounding around in our bubbled futures?
I worry about the babies, with no village to raise them.
I worry that when I am old my grandchildren
will only know me as a square on a screen.
I worry we are all nothing but internet
and open wounds, caged animals.
I am thinking about elephants.
Last year I forgot that I hated zoos
and drove 400 miles to see one.
Last year I remembered that everything could be caged, or lost
Last week I thought of an old science fiction movie I had watched
Last night I woke myself crying,
calling out over and over "Soylent Green is people."

A Casserole for Mr. Floyd

Bubbly, cheesy crust gums the side of each casserole dish,
oozes like the earnestness of strangers and extended family,
looks of polite concern pasted over faces clouded with confusion.
Hands laden with hot dishes, they arrive in caravans, carloads,
bringing coffee, punch, flowers wrapped in grocery store cellophane.

Sympathy cards crowd the mantel. Guests crowd the kitchen,
the dining room, the living room sofa, the love seat,
perch on the arms of the armchairs in twos and threes,
talk in low whispers with George's name.
The evening hangs like a young girl's bedsheet,
rippling across the sky in gauche pastel colors.

Guests serve the food. No, no, you must sit.
Guests do the dishes. No, no, you must visit family.
Guests tidy after themselves. Oh, no, we insist.
You have had such a difficult *day*.

Put your feet up. Let us get your house slippers. Don't get up.
We'll let ourselves out. Get some rest, Ms. Washington.
Go, tuck little Gianna in; tell her Daddy is sending love from heaven.

Surely someone will stop by again tomorrow.

We are so very, very sorry.

Faith

Elusive morning silence sipped by my ears
in hushed admiration.
Wind seeking the slivers of skin between my coat
and tendrils of bed-tousled hair,
mind seeking something beyond the wind,
beyond the faint trilling of birdsong,
between the crushing urgency of cars
charging toward their calendar-encapsulated days.

Eyes closed, the orange-white silhouette of the sun
burns through my eyelids,
comes on languidly, a sweet-hot apricot tinged syrup
infusing my fascia.

Gilded moment of connection.

My mind pours forth the questioning,
questing torrent, the whys and wondering,
searching for signs, or maybe just sympathy.
After the rush of words, the true entreaty,
wordless – for contentment, for peace. I wait in silence.

Only the silence answers.

to the white boy who asked me "what are you?" when we were 11 years old

If you tried to look me up
in a dictionary, searched every page,
scoured old manuscripts, unrolled papyrus
back to the ages of the disciples and fishes and loaves,
crawled through dusty low-scraping grottos
towards the innards of ancient pyramids to
scry the hieroglyphs of ages, never would you
see me rendered, never find any tongue or translation
to describe me, for I am untranslatable,
my body the unutterable truth of the generations
of queens turned to slaves, of shamans and
seers turned dime-store hustlers, yet who
in the glimmering nights held one another
like diamonds, unwilling to relinquish
what they know is priceless.

The language of your ancestors
cannot hold my own. Fraught with
Freudian slips and poor transcriptions,
your limited vowel roundness cannot
contain the singsong lilt, the cheeky click and
clack of my greatest grandparents.
Yet even among the wilderness
of your willful ignorance, some syllables
still speak volumes, that low rolling
growl in the back of our throats
which warns you that a caged soul
does not remain caged forever.
And in the end the honeyed
tang of our unfettered voices pouring
across our lips will be sweeter
than any vengeance.

Memoir of a Body

Listen, this is a Body's tell-tale voice;
six fleshy pounds born tawny-brown to a fresh-faced mama
and a faithless blue-black daddy already half-packed.

Mouth, hungry to fill the empty, grew into
toddler arms plump and round as dinner rolls,
trying to outpace the attention they were paid.

How quickly Body came to understand
the safety and shame of pillowed flesh,
and Body built a wall of wordless no.

But silent words mean nothing under dark
so when husky whispers spoke Body's name
and warned it to stay silent as stone,

Though little legs screamed for flight,
Body rose as bidden, laid upon an altar hard as death
where Body's husk was claimed both prize and sacrifice.

In preschool, already knowing the safety of solitude
Body paced the playground perimeter, fingers fluttered
plucking morning glories from their diamond prisons.

In kindergarten, the sitter's teenage son had treasures
in his room far down the hall, bought for the cost of a yes.
And Body realized what value lay within her flesh.

Beleaguered Body sought relief, found it in furtive voracity
and bloomed like giant mushrooms plumping in dark caves
subsisting on nothing but spun sugar and air.

Over years Body broadened, outward echo of inner misery,
sagging atop the thrift store jeans and too-tight shirts,
shadows concealing where childhood memory ought to be.

Thin-skinned Body felt the gaze of others grow
a weight heavier than its own prodigious flesh.
So Body sought new ways to disappear:

Stomach dissected, intestines removed, a jigsaw of mortification.
Soon Body measured success with fingers wrapped around wrists,
in watching skin pull tight to collarbones, ribs, and hips.

Thinner, then still thinner, Body still couldn't escape the gaze,
legs and breasts once buried now drew unwanted attention,
And again Body fled from the burden of male desire.

Soon crooks of elbows combed for one holy uncollapsed vein,
months turned to years, until battered Body's nervous system
shook the crumbling skeleton, a vacant-eyed rag doll.

Abscessed, dying, Body surrendered.
Defeatedly staggering into a room of other war-torn bodies,
ears slowly learning to hear, Body even more slowly came to believe.

Once a ghost town, full of blood dust and scarred bones,
Body began to fill with its own spirits, inhabit itself,
to listen to the songs of her true ancestors.

Listen, this is a tell-tale, of a Body born, then lost to itself,
at last filled with its own heart, lungs, connective tissue,
with space for the woman who had always been seeking home.

On Trich

For Noelle

[**trichotillomania** [trik-uh-til-uh-mey-nee-uh] *noun.*
a mental disorder that involves recurrent, irresistible urges
to pull out hair from your scalp, eyebrows or other areas of
your body, despite trying to stop.]

Unheeded
    fingertips inch inexorably
towards the tug
    autonomous creatures
        begging for a sense
of purpose
    to grasp, to pull,
        to urgently release from
the stubbornly selfish root
        an anti-sensation
then fleeting reprieve

    the intellect,
a hovering specter,
    oversees the effort in
        detached perplexity
held suspended
        it too is pulled
    if not physically
        then between the knowing
and the needing
    (between a groove now become a trench
        now become the San Andreas)
    encountering a peak insurmountable
as Mount Everest
    it remains transfixed
        and impotent

while animate hands
    unchecked
      stray fingers
  trace slender plots
    of destruction in their wake
        almost insignificant
aside the weeping gouges
    that shame
    that defeat
have carved,
    thoroughly concealed,
     on the insides
of the skin

The Galaxy That Swallowed Me
From the Inside Out

Sometime last night
in between
my after-dinner cigarette
and bedtime
I swallowed a galaxy.

I first felt it
as a glottal stop,
inhalation and exhalation paused,
while it inched, python-like,
past my pharynx, squeezed down my esophagus,
popping from the bottom like a cap gun,
swelling in my stomach like an overripe melon,
before lodging, creaking and expansive,
against the inside of my ribcage,
stretching it's spiral arms up the curve of my backbone,
halo tickling the tip of my uvula.

This astronomical invasion
pinned me breathless and wheezy
to the disheveled sheets of my queen bed,
gasses ballooning through my organs,
muscles bourgeoned by the gravity of
blue stars and red dwarfs, the orbits
of universes pinging against my skeleton,
nebulae oozing between my fascia,
mute and wild-eyed, blanched with a dread
only one who's body is being
endlessly expanded can fathom.

Witness to this dread and wonder,
I could no longer see the white fault lines
of my water-stained ceiling,
no longer hear the muted calling
of my family from the next room,
as I dissolved finally into the black-hole heart
of the galaxy that swallowed me from the inside out,
my vision filled with circumgalactic stardust

and the void.

an insider's guide to surviving a miscarriage

- let someone bring you endless cups
  of peppermint or raspberry tea
- let sobs escape from between
  your spasming ribs like jumping billiards
- don't apologize for matted hair or
  the open graves of your two bruised eyes
- keep the lights off
- remember the small shoes
  tucked at the back of the closet
- give your baby a name
  whisper it in the dark
  over and over like a rosary
- don't say it was your fault
- don't answer when an aunt
  or cousin or coworker call
- fuck anyone who says you can
  always try again
- fuck anyone who says
  at least you weren't further along
- turn off the phone
- remember to recite your baby's name
- keep it on the tip of the tongue
  like honey to sweeten the tea
- never let the tea go cold

still life with baby shoes

blue
with white embroidery around the cuffs
laces just for show tied into
tiny, perfect bows

the miniature shoes sit
atop the dresser, layered in dust
behind crumpled tissues, her unworn watch,
prescription bottles, long emptied

almost concealing
the crumpled ultrasound photos,
dated ten months
prior

Silence Is So Accurate

After Mark Rothko and Diane Seuss

my throat swollen
to anaphylaxis by all I have
swallowed in this lifetime,
whole sharp-edged truths,
indigestible images,
sides of the trachea
raw and rubbing together
like a surgeon's eager hands,
so close, that nothing, not sound,
not air, can birth its way
through my papered lips.

conditioned to the muzzle
my own song
only sometimes is heard
in the eerie inner throbbing
of stillness.

canary

i was eleven years old the first time my mother took me to see a therapist. we talked and talked, but she heard nothing but my words. decades flown by, i yearn a return to my eleven-year-old self. yearn to whisper back half the century to my mother's ear, guiding her to clasp my hand and lead me to the wise women, shamans and elders of our native and african ancestors with their ancient ways. shaking their heads and clucking their tongues, those sage old crones would have seated my budding body by their banked fires to warm my thick bones, heads bobbing in agreement. they would have coaxed me to drink the teas that loosen the tongues of all terrorized eleven-year-old girls, releasing my trembling voice from the box of its bone cage, vocals swooping up my throat like a canary fleeing a toxic mine. oh, how that bird-girl song would have looped among the rafters, enthralling the shamans with tales of truth and sorrow. oh, how its cloistered wings would have flapped and fluttered as it crooned a forlorn chorus. and when that canary trill quieted at last, its windpipe dry and scraped raw, how they would have plucked it up and cupped it tenderly in weathered palms, dripped warm salves of nectars and herbs down its aching throat, and placed it back upon my chest where i lay asleep curled among the other children and hunting hounds in a great circular pile around the fire. those elder women would be watching over my slumbering bird-girl form, nodding to themselves and each other, knowing that tomorrow, i would sing again, and the next day, and the day after that, and at each singing, my feathered voice growing sweet and strong, they would grin their wide, toothless grins.

sink

I sit at my kitchen sink.
Water sluices down my arms, over my thighs,
spills over the countertops, puddles on the floor
where someone will have to mop it up later.
I sit at the kitchen sink, as steamy water turns pink,
then blooms a crimson blaze of fireworks,
gurgles, a slow spring brook, as it pools
from wrists to palms, cupped to slake a thirst.
I sit at my kitchen sink and stare out the window,
watch tangerine leaves plummet with the fall wind
as the woman down the street walks by
with her lab puppy straining at its leash,
and I sit at my kitchen sink
as the warm water starts to run cold,
and I see my neighbor pull into our shared driveway,
move my forearms onto my goose-fleshed thighs
smearing the stainless steel into ruby still life
watch as he walks from his car with bags
full of the week's groceries and into his house,
his back porch flooded bright until his door closes.
He turns off the light.

On That Day, February 2014

Each day as I walked to your room, with its nameplate decorated
with ribbons and tiny pom-poms, you asked me for ice cream.
Each time, I reminded you that ice cream would not tolerate
the twenty-minute drive from my house, but that you could ask
the staff for a little cup of vanilla or chocolate. Then, you would beg
for root beer. Dutifully I would trudge down the long industrial corridor
to the nurse's lounge for the one drink not on your menu.
That day, you did not ask for root beer. That day, you did not ask
for anything. Lying peacefully in your hospital bed,
you looked as if you were napping, but stayed motionless
as I took your hand. Your eyelids fluttered wildly, as if in dream,
your breath a startling gurgle in the silence. They told me to expect that,
the death rattle. I talked to you, a little, and then I was silent too, wondered
if you could hear anything I said. After some time, I decided
it did not matter and spoke again. I told you I love you.
I told you I love you again. I told you the truth, about everything.
About why I'd been so angry with you before I went to rehab.
How it had never been your fault, always mine; how now
I could finally admit it. How I wished you had been able to stay
longer, to see me in recovery, see me alive. I made you promises,
ones I've never told another soul. But I'll always keep. In the end,
when the rattle came less and less, I told you I'd never wanted
any other mother but you. And you breathed in.
And I held your hand tighter.

Letter to My Mother in Winter

It's early this year
  the snow falling
 before Halloween
heavy as unshared burdens
    I feel it in my elbow first
     (the one I broke falling down
  the stairs another Winter years ago
       when you drove an hour to see me in the hospital)
that familiar dull pull on the regrown bone
    as I carry the groceries in through
   the slush to our bright blue kitchen

  The snowy season is when I miss you most
    when I recall the festive times
the traditions you tried so hard
     to instill like guard rails
       against the tornado of your family legacy
   the women's hushed gossip
in the kitchen as they washed
     dishes after every holiday meal
    – making a fallacy of any feminist protestations

  The walls, the season, remind me
of the way you painted
   our old kitchen avocado green
    trimmed in white, perfectly decorated for the holiday parties
   you hosted, where we'd decorate dozens of cookies and candies
marzipan, fudge, spritz, divinity, gingerbread
    lining every countertop

Still, as I put away the flour, butter, sugar
for my own upcoming baking day
I love you best for this – that in every
perfectly crafted confection, every familial recipe
you wrote out by hand, passed down
on index cards in your flowered green box
I could read within your thin, delicate scrawl
this, daughter, is not
the only way it's done

Body Language

It speaks to me each morning, telling me
I have been alive for five decades. Whispers
sigh in my inner ear so that words others speak
come to me softened, sometimes incoherent.
Sprouts of silvered hair line the curve
of my jaw, where I persistently pluck the white tips
in tight-lipped defiance. We are locked
in a conversation, my flesh and I,
about the passage of time.

Like a stranger in someone else's home,
I am yoked inside an assemblage of organs,
a hermit shell I've hungered to shed,
pulse a pace I did not set. Yet I wander
it's spiraled halls, calling my own name
just to hear it's murmured echo, seeking
its conched heart, hoping still,
for any kind of refuge.

Language Does the Best It Can

some languages have multiple
words for every type of love;
but some have none.
what trust is there in faulty vocabularies
moored years in our brains,
ships with a thousand anchors.
how can we surrender, unafraid,
to this peculiar phenomenon,
unacquainted with its fleeting pulse,
not knowing its nature,
not knowing how to let the heart
skip a beat without stopping
to catch our breath.
how can we speak, unknowing
if to say the words
I love you
are the same as saying
I was incomplete
without you.

Unscripted

Standing in my kitchen, dicing beets and rutabaga for dinner,
I am struck by a sudden and unfamiliar sense of *rightness*.

* * *

As a young girl with fingernails caked from sunbaked mud pies,
a woman's sophistication was tied with strings of aprons and pear
a man's relaxation found shaken not stirred,
followed by a gentle cigar puff.
My sacred teachings softly offered from June or Carol Ann rerun
Life, sweet and succinct, was framed by commercial breaks,
and words from our saintly sponsors.

Eventually my sprouting pigtails escaped
from their elasticized bondage.
Pouty pubescent lips glazed in Baby Soft lip gloss,
Brady Bunch dreams replaced by *Charlie's Angels*,
a yearning for that worldly, polyester-clad charisma,
a life of independence, adventure, intrigue, the ultimate escape.

* * *

But life being life, roads being roads, prone to potholes or detour
I stumbled and tumbled my way to adulthood –
landing bare butt-cheeked against the cold linoleum
of my tiny efficiency bathroom, wailing alone
over two faint fuchsia lines, crushed by a curtain of certainty
that this was not how my life story was meant to unfold.

I had always asserted that I was much too selfish for motherhoo
And the day they swept my owl-eyed brown baby as I stared at h
in my trembling arms, I had two simultaneous thoughts:
I must care for this exquisite creature with my very life,
and,
The life I had hoped for is over.

48

From inside me, my independent Angel folded her wings,
hissing in dismay, imagining motherhood come to roost,
a homely old hen, ready to eclipse her like a gibbous moon.

And then the babe made a sound,
half pigeon coo, half owl hoot –
that clanged against my core like the clapper
of every bell in heaven,
and I cleft open like a second birthing,
so stunning my breath ensnared mid-air.
Into this raw miracle, motherhood unfolded,
no lumbering fowl, but a homey Hestia*,
hand outstretched in offering.

* * *

Returning home to my new one bedroom apartment,
squalling infant in tow, I plunged, resolute,
into an alien landscape –
sagging cities of burp rags, trails of ride-along toys,
gardens of board books –
hardly noticing the lessening press of Hestia's hand
with each tantrum,
of hers,
or mine.

Caught in this daily Dreft-doused wash cycle,
dreams of a life of painting, poetry, travel, intrigue
drawn down by the albatross of my anxiety.
Big girl panties and ballet lessons, a white room
painted pink, then blue, then black, then back to white,
homework folders checked nightly, and a relentless guilt
for the third boxed dinner that week.
Yet somehow, together, we grew up.

* * *

So, life is still life, and roads still roads,
and still I stumble and fumble.
But I am barefoot and bustling in my new two-bedroom apartmen
college homework temporarily set aside with paint-dappled hand
and as I slide oil-shined vegetables into the oven,
dinner for the mini-me planted belly-to-carpet, chin in hand
eyes unblinkingly locked on a blue screen flickering scenes of he
own presumed womanhood.

And I am struck by how the mundanity of my devotion
had transformed my universe – as it dawned on me how
I was always the author, and there was never a script needed.

*Hestia was the virgin goddess of Hearth & Home, one of the Olympi
Deities. Refusing all proposals of marriage, she asked Zeus for etern
maidenhood. Her hearth was essential for warmth, food preparation, and sh
oversaw all sacrificial offerings to deities.

Visitor

when contentment
flies to your soul
let it
let it be
a winged thing
come to greet you
in your hallway
on the way to the bathroom
in the early morning
in the gauzy afternoons
when you are grudgingly walking the dog

let it greet you, a cheerful ghost
kissing both cheeks
pass through the cloud
of its crisp greeting
and let the unfamiliar shiver
slip down your spine
grab the tail of it like
the string of a lost
balloon.
don't
let go.

Starting with We

In homage to Marge Piercy

Lover approaches my chair from behind
lifts my hair from my neck, kissing the
spot just below my right ear soft as a
hummingbird's kiss, softer than a
spring fog in Maine, whispers words
of devotion into my skin as if it
were a confessional booth. My hands,
poised over the keyboard, pause,
and then resume their typing as
I lean my body gently away from
their buttery lips. I am too busy,
I tell them, for such shenanigans,
but heat is burning in through my
solar plexus and my pulse
is in my eardrums
like an ultrasound wave.

Each morning, after swallowing
my 200 mg of hope down with a glass
of water, I say my prayers to
the Universe that today will be
the day I am not afraid. Today, I will
reach for my lover's hand first, kiss each
one of their fingertips in soft-eyed sanctity,
unleery and open as a fault line,
welcoming intimacy as oblate,
prayers of gratitude sweetening
the meeting of our wanting mouths.

Ex Gratia

I am uploading my new engagement photos.
Thoughtlessly using the same app that you and I
used all those years ago, the one that lets you
create your fantasy wedding and website. It's true,
machines have memories longer than elephants,
and as I open it the screen stubbornly flashes your name
in twenty-four-point font across the ornate scrollwork headline.
My fingers click the mouse furiously, back, back, back
arrow to find the offending field still carrying your name
before my fiancé's attention shifts away from their work,
over to my screen. It is not as if we have not all acknowledged you,
haven't all become a strange little family: me and my fiancé,
you and your husband, the five of us
(with the ghost of our relationship past)
together at Christmas over baked ham and sweet potatoes.
Swatting the mosquitos away from each other at summer BBQs.
Folding each other's laundry over Starbucks and home baked treats.
And I would be lying if I didn't say I don't think about the future – you
as guest at my wedding, all of us grown old and grizzled together.
How you and I had once pictured the front porch, the rocking chairs.
How the view has changed since you lived here.

Aubade for a New World

You pour cream into your coffee,
just a splash, cooling it to a dark sorrel
before handing me my caramel colored cup,
and we crawl back into bed to ward off
the chill of a hard hibernal morning –
if only for a few more minutes.
We are talking of babies;
whether you, who had your breasts
removed last year, can possibly endure
the growing of a child in an organ you'd
so often wished you could expunge like a birth.
I am too old, we both know. But you,
sixteen years my junior, are
fertile as the moon
is now full.

Coffee forgotten on the nightstand,
You tell me... yes.
                              Yes.

I and U and I

"I have always known that at last I would take this road, but
yesterday, I did not know that it would be today."
—Narihara

We pull into the parking lot.
You turn off the engine.
Heat builds to a boil in the closed cab,
but neither of us move to open the doors.
I cover your hand with mine and squeeze,
and finally you turn your head towards mine.
We kiss, chastely, mouths closed in solemnity.
Hands clasped like timid kindergartners on a first day at school,
we head towards the clinic entrance.

The receptionist is kind but no nonsense,
directs us to wait for the nurse.
The nurse comes out to the waiting room,
calls out your deadname.
I squeeze your hand harder.

We follow back to the exam room.
Nurse chipperly explains the procedure,
as if we haven't researched and talked
and dreamed of it for months.
She asks us to confirm the donor number
on the small white vial waiting on the counter.
She leaves.

You undress from the waist down,
leaving on your Captain America socks,
climb atop the table and into the stirrups.
The nurse practitioners enter.
They chipperly explain the procedure, confirm the donor.

You lie back on the table, covered in paper sheets.
The speculum slips inside, followed by the catheter,
and lastly, the sample.
I scan your face, pinched in discomfort, the entire time.
I am watching to see if you have left your body,
or if you are still with me.
In two minutes, it is over.

They give us follow-up instructions,
set a timer for ten minutes, and leave.
We chat faleteringly, fall into silence,
my head on your chest on the table.

The timer goes off, and I help you get dressed.
We head back to the car, hands vined again, tighter now,
as if holding hope in our joined hands.

Sliver

Like pieces
of a fractured mirror,
I carry your broken
heart, slivered into
the deepest, hot-pink tissue
of my own. I carry your splintered
heart like a sliver, scarred around
with ropy muscle, pulsing in time
with my pulse, not yours.
I carry the slivers
like shrapnel, healed over,
only felt when moving,
when breathing too deeply.
When they say time heals
all wounds that is to say
time buries, time
inters all pieces
of the heart I carry,
shivved into my own
beating, heaving
heart.

Shorn

This infinite memory multiplies
by decades, clings like debris
on sheep too long unshorn,
suffocating, snagged along
mountain paths on their
trudge towards certitude.

I beg to be razed, stripped to a *tabula rasa*,
relieved of my duty to witness.
Let me be a babe, skin goose-fleshed in new air,
achingly cold, beautifully unchained.

At 48

And now
I become myself;
a hardened
bulb of dahlia
buried under
winter's compacted earth.

Swelling with sun,
I break apart into breathing tendrils
seeking the living air.

Bare and hot,
I raise my petaled head
and bow to the wind,
my only master.

Clutter

The top of a well-loved desk
is a living organism,
a mélange of odd organs preserved in a skin of dust,
an abandoned wristwatch sluggishly ticking its heartbeat,
the hollowed stomach of cooled coffee cups,
streeted veins on a time-worn map faded in the slanting sunlight
the flashbulb memories of curled yellow snapshots,
a jumble of *carpe kairos*,
testament of days where luck
flowed in, and days
where it hemorrhaged out again,
freckled with the accumulated coins, pins, clips, and caps
in ceremonial adornment.
This holy altar of sacred ordinary objects,
skeletons of life lived, and life taken, arranged
in a perfect toss of God's heavenly dice.

The Good Truth

It is no accident, that when you look back
at old photos, the ones you first shunned
(thighs too fat, hair too messy)
showing your round-eyed daughter
what life was like back then, that you see yourself
differently. See there, how you threw back your head
with laughter, mouth sheltered by one slender hand.
See how your eyes were full and soft as a mare's,
how once you were unseasoned. How easy
it is to forget you are her. How easy, to forget
that it all belongs to you – the laughter,
the innocence, the fight, the ache –
how it is yours as the moon is the tide's:
an uncountable distance away,
but always there, in your
hollow, cupped hands.

Aubade to the Sacred

Up before the household, the dark hours of the morning
are mine. Littered in routine – coffee, meds, emails –
this is my hallowed litany each dawn.

Every morning as I prepare, I pass the etched glass plate
rescued from my grandmother's estate, a background of
green
flowing behind her graceful form, swirl of black hair
touching earth, she surveys me in mute benediction.
She is my Kuan Yin, my goddess of compassion,
an *aide-mémoire* of some long-ago grace.

I walk into the hazy sun lit garden,
to the aqua blue hammock, lower myself into it,
a bowing before communion, then lie silent
in watery illumination, listening to early birdsong.
Hands open, I pray for her to bless this new day.

Today

First let your mutable body
lie down in some untamed place,
let it find an imprint
among the dirt, the ants, the grass,
knowing that it knows
how to return to this womb
of its own accord,
knowing that it knows the grass
like the skin of a lover,
softer than suede, damp
with earthen excitement
at the sun's dewy blessing.
Now let your fingers trace
the braille bark of a branch,
let the feel of the warm wood
under your touch
tell you what it is
to be embodied. Lie still,
understanding that one day,
the earth will hold you closer
than your own skin,
knowing that today is not that day.

Acknowledgments

This book could not have come to fruition without the support of so many generous souls. To begin with, I want to acknowledge the patience of my beloved spouse Dannee and daughter Noelle. Without their constant tolerance of my obsession with the writing and editing process, and willingness to be my first audience, nothing would make it onto the page. Next, I want to call out to the many others who listen to, give feedback on, and encourage my writing, including Stephanie T., Emily H., Anna D., Mary W., and Lisa Marie B. I value them all so much. And lastly, my neverending gratitude to the whole team at Cornerstone Press, including Dr. Ross Tangedal, Grace Dahl, Brett Hill, and Julia Kaufman, and their design and editing teams. You have all truly helped me transform this manuscript into a book of which I can truly be proud. Thank you, all, for believing in me.

Gratefully acknowledged are the following publications, where particular poems appeared in earlier forms:

"Traditions," "Schools," "At 48," and "The Good Truth" first appeared in *The Good Truth* © 2021 Finishing Line Press.

"Second Harvest" first appeared in *Literary Mama*, and then in *The Good Truth* © 2021 Finishing Line Press.

"Shorn" first appeared as part of The Journey Project © 2021 *Floresta Magazine*.

"to the white boy who asked me 'what are you?' when we were 11 years old" first appeared in a slightly different version in *Cutleaf Literary Journal*.

"Metamorphosis" appeared in the March 29, 2022, edition of *Maya's Micros/The Closed Eye Open*.

"Eight and a Half Lilies in October" appeared in the March 2022 issue of *The Burrow Press Review*.

"At 48" and "Today" appeared in *The Hyacinth Review*.

"The Galaxy That Swallowed Me from the Inside Out" first appeared in the July 2022 issue of *Strange Horizons*.

The poems "Aubade to a New World", "I and U and I", and "Starting with We" are forthcoming in issue 48.2 of *Obsidian*.

"an insider's guide to surviving a miscarriage" is forthcoming in the Winter issue of *CALYX Journal*.

"Ideas on Survival" and "First Smoke" appeared in the March 18, 2022 issue of *Wet Cement Press Magazine*.

"Ex Gratia" first appeared in the December 2022 issue of *The Coop: A Poetry Cooperative*.

R.B. Simon is a queer, black visual artist and writer. She has been published in multiple journals, among them *Stoneboat*, *Equinox*, *Burrow Press Review*, *Strange Horizons*, *Sky Island Journal*, *pacificREVIEW*, and *Literary Mama*. She also has upcoming work appearing in *CALYX*, *The Coop*, and *Obsidian*. Her poem "Clutter" was shortlisted for the 2022 Julia Darling Memorial Poetry Prize, and her chapbook, *The Good Truth*, published in July 2021, placed 3rd in the Wisconsin Fellowship of Poets chapbook contest. In her "free time" she enjoys reading and painting, along with her more peculiar passions, including clothing with stripes, giraffes, and coffee-flavored caffeine. She is currently living in Madison, Wisconsin, with her spouse, Dannee, young adult daughter, Noelle Elizabeth, and four unruly little dogs.